A Love Like No Other

Copyright © 2025 by Lakisha Young
All rights reserved.
ISBN: 978-1-7374371-1-6

This book or any portion thereof may not be reproduced or used in any way by any means, electronic, mechanical, photography, recording or otherwise, without the express written permission of the publisher as provided by USA copyright law. This book should not be redistributed or reproduced.

Unless otherwise indicated, Biblical quotations are taken from the New King James Version®. Copyright © 1982 by Thomas Nelson. Used by permission. All rights reserved.

Scripture quotations marked MSG are taken from THE MESSAGE, copyright © 1993, 2002, 2018 by Eugene H. Peterson. Used by permission of NavPress, represented by Tyndale House Publishers. All rights reserved.

Scripture quotations marked (NIV) are taken from the Holy Bible, New International Version®, NIV®. Copyright © 1973, 1978, 1984, 2011 by Biblica, Inc.™ Used by permission of Zondervan. All rights reserved worldwide. www.zondervan.com The "NIV" and "New International Version" are trademarks registered in the United States Patent and Trademark Office by Biblica, Inc.™

A Love Like No Other

Lakisha Young

A Love Like No Other

DEDICATION

This book is dedicated to Abba, my spiritual Father. Lord, you are the Alpha and Omega; you have been with me from the beginning, and I know you will be with me until the end. Your love, grace, and mercy for me have guided me through all these years, and for this, I am grateful. To honor Him, I dedicate this book to my Lord Jesus Christ.

CONTENTS

	Acknowledgments	i
1	My Pathway Begins	5
2	Dysfunction Begins	9
3	True Love, So I Thought	15
4	Back on the Pathway to Finding Love	26
5	Pathway of Depression	30
6	Pathway of Destruction	34
7	Moving on	48
8	From One Pathway of Destruction to Another	55
9	The Pathway of Destruction Ends	64
10	Back on the Wrong Pathway	70
11	The Pathway to God's Love	82

ACKNOWLEDGMENTS

This book was written prior to the passing of my father. Before my father passed away, he prayed the prayer of salvation and he passed away peacefully. Even though my father has passed away, I would like to thank my mother and my father for being understanding and allowing me to tell my story. We each have our testimony of how the love of God has gotten us through life's difficult challenges. God's love for us allowed us to heal, love again, and find forgiveness in our hearts. I want to thank my sons for the love we share and the close relationship we have. During my journey, God was with me and my children. As a mother, I am very proud of the godly and caring men my sons have grown to be. I also want to give special thanks to my grandchildren, who I adore and love dearly. After writing this book, God placed a wonderful and loving man in my life. I want to express my gratitude to my husband and Pastor Dr. Ramon Jones. Our union was a divine connection from God.

INTRODUCTION

Today, I am the woman whose pathway in life led to discovering and accepting God's unconditional love. I've learned to love and respect myself as a woman. But I didn't always exist as this woman. After being continuously rejected by my parents, friends and in relationships with men, I was continually looking for acceptance as a child and even in my early adult years. The experiences and feelings of repeated rejection, abandonment, and heartache caused me to feel broken. I believe brokenness in the emotional and mental sense can mean many things; however, Merriam-Webster's Dictionary says brokenness is "being damaged or altered from its original state." One may become emotionally or mentally broken by experiencing psychological distress caused by traumatic life events such as the end of a close relationship, the loss of a loved one, personal tragedy, domestic abuse, the loss of a job, and other reasons.

I longed to be accepted and loved by my parents and other individuals I encountered. However, what I thought was true love was not love at all. I thought true love would come from my parents, close friends, and the men I was involved with. I looked for love externally and through the eyes of others instead of looking for it within.

How could I expect to be loved by someone or love someone when I did not know how to love myself? How could I love myself when I did not know the love of God? My idea of love was having a physical being in your life who loves you unconditionally through the good and the bad. I came to discover that this is God's love. God is a spiritual being who loves you unconditionally, and He will "never leave us nor forsake us" (1 Kings 8:57b, NIV).

God has always been there for me and has loved me, even when I did not acknowledge or feel His love for me. God's love for me cuddled me when I felt alone and abandoned. His love for me strengthened me when I was weak and rescued me from all the bad decisions I made. "God is love, and whoever lives in love, lives in God and God lives in them" (1 John 4:16 NIV). I had been on a long path searching for true love.

It took me many years to acknowledge God's love for me. However, I did not know of God's love, and you don't know what you have not learned or been taught. I did not grow up knowing the foundational principles of true love. To navigate through life, we need a strong foundation. God's word provides a foundation that guides us in how we should go.

Psalm 119:105, NLT, expresses, "The word is the lamp to my feet and a light to my path." If I had known God's love and how much He loved me in my early years, it would not have taken me until my adult years to discover God's love, and his love is a love like no other.

CHAPTER 1

MY PATHWAY BEGINS

I am the only child of my parents. Up until my preschool years, I had a decent life. My dad was an accountant at the courthouse, and my mother worked in several different fields. Their combined incomes classified us as a middle-class family. My parents provided me with all the materialistic things a child would want and more. I knew my parents loved me. However, my parents' strongholds superseded their love for me over time.

My parents' relationship was unstable and volatile; they constantly fought physically. They would often fight, separate, and get back together. When they separated, my parents would fight about who I should live with, and I always preferred to live with my mother. I loved my mother unconditionally and was very close to her; I idolized my mother. She was beautiful, outgoing, and could not do anything wrong in my eyes. My mother was very loving; however, she disciplined me more than my father. She was the one who fussed at me or punished me. When my mother hollered out my full name, I knew I was in trouble. Sometimes, that was all she needed to do to get me to behave.

I loved my father, but I mostly viewed him as a mean man, and I was not very close to him growing up. He did not smile much, and he was rude to everyone. Even though I thought he was a very mean man, I also knew I was his baby girl, and I could do nothing wrong in his eyes. I knew my father had a gentle side to him, and he loved me dearly. However, I often saw his dark side.

As far as I could remember, my father drank a lot. His constant drinking elevated his temper and led to frequent fights with my mother. He would often blame my mother for everything that did not go the way he expected. My father did not want me to witness the arguments and fights and always yelled at me to go to my room when they argued. There were times when I witnessed my father physically abusing my mother. However, I would always hear them, and it was like I was right there with my mother as she endured it all. To make it even more evident, she would have bruises and black eyes the next day after the physical abuse.

Consequently, I did not respect my father for his behavior toward my mother. After seeing how my father treated my mother, I often said that I would never want a man in my life who displayed all his negative characteristics. Little did I know that my life path would lead me to relationships with men who mirrored some or all of my biological father's negative characteristics. There is a saying that women marry men like their fathers. However, if I had known then about God's true love, I would have married a man who resembled my spiritual father's love and positive characteristics.

As an only child, I often felt alone. I had imaginary friends, but I wanted real friends as well. However, kids did not naturally want to play with me. To get them to play with me, I would bribe them and offer to give them my toys. As a child, one does not understand why kids do not naturally want to play with each other. I did not understand why kids did not want to be my friend and play with me. This was the beginning of feeling rejected and unworthy, which continued throughout my elementary and middle school years. I grew tired of offering toys for people to be my friend and began sacrificing myself by doing things I should not have been doing.

I would do things for people to like me and become my friends. To avoid losing friends, I would do whatever was asked of me, whether right or not. I did not understand why I had to go out of my way to make friends. I would always cry about this. To make the situation worse with making friends, we were constantly moving, and I never had the opportunity to develop long-lasting friendships.

I did not grow up in the church learning the love of God or Godly principles. My mom and I only attended church on certain holidays, such as Easter, Mother's Day, and Christmas. Growing up, my parents also did not teach me the value of self-worth or self-love. But how could I be taught these foundational principles or values when my parents were not exposed to them growing up? These feelings or behavior patterns were passed down from generation to generation

CHAPTER 2

DSYFUNCTION BEGINS

Both of my parents grew up in a single-parent home. My mother was the fourth child out of five children. My mother was not close with my maternal grandmother. She lived with her aunt as a child and then moved home with her mother when she got older. My mother did not have many pleasant memories of living with her mother. Her mother also displayed addictive behaviors, and this was an added level of living in a home not centered on love. My mother revealed that she did not feel loved by her father, who was absent for most of her life.

My father was the oldest of five children. My father always talked about the negative environment he lived in, and he did not feel like he was loved growing up. He felt his mother loved his siblings more than she loved him. Similarly, to my mother's father, my father's father was also absent from his life. However, his stepfather was in his life, but my father revealed he was an alcoholic and was drunk most of the time.

My parents came from dysfunctional families and then built a dysfunctional family of their own. My mom and dad both felt unloved by one or both of their parents. I understand that it is difficult to give something you never had or teach something you were never exposed to. Because of this, I was not taught about true love or how to love myself.

With my parents going through their tumultuous relationship, they focused less on me. This allowed me to be free and do whatever I wanted, but I often felt abandoned and unloved. When my mother used to go out and party a lot, she would leave me at home alone or take me to my aunt's house. Though I was at my aunt's house, there was not much parental supervision either because my aunt would go out just as much as my mother. My cousins and I were unsupervised, so we would always have people over or stay out late at night.

As a preteen, I gave more of myself to make friends, but I was not establishing genuine friendships. I was teased a lot, and it always felt like I was not good or pretty enough. I also did not know how to stand up for myself. When my friends came over to visit me, my father would question everyone, or he would slam the door on them and then tell me someone was at the door for me. Because of my father's demeanor, my friends did not want to come to visit or spend the night at my house. This situation also made it difficult to keep friends.

I became interested in boys at a very young age, but my parents had different mindsets about my interest. My mother did not mind when I shared that I liked a boy or had a boyfriend. However, my dad was ultimately against the idea of me being interested in boys. Even though I was interested in boys, they did not always show it or they would tease me. Being teased by boys and my friends enhanced my feelings of unworthiness and low self-esteem. When boys did show interest, I felt like the only way to keep them was to make out with them. This led to me having a negative reputation as the girl who was "easy." It was difficult to be known as "easy" while simultaneously hiding the truth that my life was anything but a yellow brick road and very complicated.

During middle school, my life began to turn for the worst. It became a normal routine for my mom to party and stayed out all night. When she returned, she and my father would have physical fights. My mother lost her job during this time, which created financial struggles for our house. There were many times we were without lights or phone service because the bills were not paid. There were also times when we did not have groceries. My father became the sole provider, but I do not think he managed this responsibility well.

On one occasion, my mother went to the grocery store and did not return. I worried and waited hours for her to walk through the doors of our home. When my father finally returned home, he told me my mother went to jail for theft. I was devastated. How could my mother get caught up in a situation that would take her away from me? I felt alone and abandoned by my mother and blamed my father for everything happening.

Unfortunately, my mother was in jail for several months. My dad was not able to handle things financially so he began selling our furniture to have money to pay the bills. We also moved out of our home and into a small three-bedroom apartment with my mother's older sister. My mother was eventually released from jail, and five of us lived in my aunt's three-bedroom apartment. At the time, I did not understand why things were happening the way they were.

Things continued to get worse because both of my parents were unemployed. My father was permanently suspended from his job because he had many occasions when he arrived to work drunk or with a hangover. Also, my parents' drug addiction became very apparent during this time. My mother had not worked for a while, but she would go on binges and be gone for days. My father would be present, but he would be bingeing in the bathroom. Why were my parents putting me through all this pain and suffering? I had so many unanswered questions.

It was hard to understand where my parents were in their lives. Questions about how my parents got to this horrible place in their lives or how their negative behaviors became more important than caring for and loving me filled my mind. Because I did not understand or have any answers to these questions, I felt so unloved and cried all the time. They were no longer in a state to provide for me or love me the way parents were supposed to provide for and love their children. At that time, their addiction was greater than their love for me. But I had no idea I was God's child. I did not know it, but He was right there by my side, loving me and guiding me through these difficult times. I wished I had known about His love and accepted it back then. If I had, I would have avoided the path of painful mistakes in trying to find the love in the wrong places.

Growing up, every child expects a life of love from their parents. No child anticipates being neglected or feeling abandoned by their parents. No child anticipates growing up with parents showing physical abuse or becoming addicted to drugs. As a child, you question, "What did I do wrong?" and "How could I fix the problem?" As a child, you do not know the importance of reaching out to others for support or looking up tools or strategies for dealing with parents who are addicted. You learn about these things as you get older. As a child, you are not equipped to handle such despair. Most of the time, these negative experiences impact us in negative ways that guide how we grow as adults. For some, we become victims of our upbringing. For others, we grow with time and learn how to handle and cope with such situations.

The key to overcoming the neglect and abandonment that lead to brokenness is knowing the love of God and what His word says about love. Unfortunately, we do not come into the world knowing who God is and how much He loves us, no matter what we are born into or experience at the beginning of life. If I had come into existence knowing the word of God and how much He loved me, I would have been crying out to Him for understanding. I would have been praying to Him to heal me in my brokenness. I would have been journaling about my experiences and emotions and seeking His guidance by reading His words daily.

CHAPTER 3

TRUE LOVE, SO I THOUGHT

We lived with my aunt for a little over a year. I don't know if we were evicted or if my parents and aunt just agreed and decided to go their separate ways. My parents also separated and went their separate ways. My parents never tried to get back together after this last separation. During this last separation, it appeared that my dad had just walked away from his responsibilities easily, without a care of how this was affecting me. However, I really did not care much because I was with my mother.

Unfortunately, living with my mother was not the best situation. My mother moved us into a duplex that was deplorable. Living the way we were living was the reality of how my mother's drug addiction began to take over her life and how she began to focus less on caring for me. It was normal for me to feel alone because my mother was not there for me, and I did not have anyone to confide in. As throughout my years, I often found myself crying and feeling sad. Then one day the clouds lifted, and I met a young man who I thought was my saving grace. I thought I was being rescued from my sad and depressing life.

I will call him "the Provider" because I thought he was my savior and would provide for me in all the ways my parents failed. Based on my definition of a savior, I thought he would save me from the life I was living and give me the love and provision I needed. The Provider was a very nice and sweet young man. He was very supportive of me and attentive to my needs, especially knowing what I was going through with my mother.

I was 14 years old when I met him. I knew he was older than me, so I did not tell him the truth about how old I was. However, later in the relationship, I had no choice but to tell him the truth. After dating for several months, I became pregnant. Becoming pregnant at the age of 14 was not the best decision. However, I was very excited about being pregnant. I would have someone to show my love and love me back in return.

His mother was adamant about us marrying, whereas my mother was initially opposed. But I convinced her that this was what I wanted. My mother and I had to go to the courthouse for my mother to sign over her parental rights for me to become an emancipated minor. Despite her apprehension, she agreed and decided to give up her parental rights. What parent in their right mind does that? But my mother was not in a state of mind where she was making the right decisions. However, I was glad she agreed to sign me over. I thought the only way to a new beginning of love and happiness was to get out of my mother's neglect and exposure to her addiction. Unfortunately, I was so wrong.

After my mom signed me over, I moved in with the Provider and his parents. I was so happy to be away from my mother. My father and I had not spoken much, aside from me sharing with him that I was pregnant. He stated that he was very disappointed in me and did not want to have anything to do with me. How dare he become disappointed with me, considering what I had to endure from him as a father? He did not provide for me or love me as a father should. He did not teach me about self-love or values that would have guided me to make better decisions in life.

The Provider and I got married three months before my first son was born. The Provider and I did have premarital counseling before our wedding. However, the pastor advised that we were not ready and did not truly understand what marriage was about. I was not raised on God's word about marriage. Nor did I grow up around positive representations of a kingdom marriage. Even though I did not know what true love was, I thought I was in love, and against the pastor's advice, we proceeded to get married.

For the moment, I was in a happy and blissful place. I was married and believed I had discovered true love. To make this moment even more special, my first son was born; it was a joyous occasion. It is amazing how new life can bring people back together. Everyone was at the hospital celebrating the birth of my son. Even my father was there; considering, I had not spoken to him since I informed him of my pregnancy. It was amazing how this little bundle of joy brought everyone out of their negative feelings or situations to come together and celebrate God's creation.

Unhappy in love

It did not take long for me to discover the life I was living, was not going to bring me the happiness and love I was seeking. I loved my son dearly; however, I was unhappy being married. I was living an adult life without having experienced life as an average teenager. I thought being with the Provider would compensate for the abandonment and feelings of neglect that I had experienced in my earlier years. I thought his love for me was all I needed, but it was not.

How could I accept and appreciate his love when I still did not know how to love myself? I still felt unworthy and unloved because I had not dealt with all the emotional pain that I had endured from my parents. I was not exposed to positive depictions of true love and marriage as a child. The depictions of marriage I was exposed to frequently included abuse, addiction, and adultery.

Both of my parents had affairs outside of their marriage. As horrible as this may appear, I was upset when I found out my father cheated, but was accepting of my mother cheating. I thought the world of my mother. I thought she had the right to cheat because of how my father treated her. Since I idolized my mother and she could do no wrong in my eyes, I thought that was the standard. One year after being married, I cheated on my husband.

At this point in my journey, I was a 16-year-old girl in 10th grade, wanting friends but not having any. I remember not fitting in with my classmates because I was married and had a son. However, one young man had my attention, and I had his. He was very handsome, with light brown eyes, and very charming. I was very surprised that he showed interest in me. I was very flattered and did not care about the fact that I was married with a son. We started with having friendly conversations, but those friendly conversations led to a romantic relationship. I knew being with this young man was wrong, but I did it anyway.

As much as I wanted to be loved and cried about it in my early years, I did not know how to love. How could I have known what true love was when I came from a broken family, and our family dynamics were not centered around love? I tried very hard to be the Provider's wife and love him as a wife should love her husband. The more I tried to love him, the more miserable I became.

Eventually, I came to my senses and wanted to do the right thing. I knew being married and having an affair was not the right thing to do, even if I was unhappy. Because of this, I ended the relationship with that young man. I confessed my sins to my husband; he forgave me and decided we would continue working on our marriage.

Repeated Behavior

During my junior year of high school, I decided to transfer to a school near my maternal grandmother because they had an onsite daycare for students. This was a great benefit for students who had kids because it allowed them to continue their education and not withdraw from school because of teen pregnancy.

I did not know how to drive or have a car at the time, so my husband and I decided I would live with my grandmother during the week and come home on the weekend. When I first started school, my mother was living with my grandmother. However, she continued to go on her binges and be gone for weeks.

During the first half of 11th grade, I struggled because I was not focused on school. I wanted to be independent and make my own money. I did not want to be dependent on my husband financially. I worked at night at a fast-food restaurant. As a result, I either missed school or slept in class. My grades suffered, but this did not last long. When it came to school or my career, there was something within me that wanted more or wanted me to do the right thing. I believe these feelings were from God covering and loving me. He'd let me go down the wrong path for a while, but He'd eventually pull me back onto the right one. From the feelings within, I decided to quit my job and take school seriously.

Though I excelled in school, I continued to be unhappy in my marriage. I believe I was a great teenage mom. However, as teenagers do, I wanted to hang out with other people. So again, I found myself in another relationship outside of my marriage. Once again, my behavior was reckless for a married woman. As a result, my husband was fed up with my behavior and put me out of the house. I did not care at the time because my friend's mom allowed me to move into their home.

My friend was also a young mother, and we were always together with our kids. She would keep my son when I went out and vice versa. This was fun for a while, but it did not last. I was still a married woman, and what I was doing was not right. Once again, God allowed me to go astray for a little while before he pulled me back on the right path. I pleaded with my husband, and he forgave me. I eventually moved back home with him.

When I first moved home, everything was going well between my husband and me. We were working on improving our marriage. Several months later, I became pregnant with my second son. This happened right before my senior year. I had learned how to drive, and my husband bought me a car. I did not have to move back with my grandmother because I was able to drive back and forth to school. Things were continuing to go well; I was the wife and mother I needed to be, and we were excited and anticipating the birth of my second son.

My second son was born two months before my graduation from high school. Graduation was a proud moment for me. I graduated with honors, and most importantly, my parents attended. I had a proud moment after having another son and graduating with honors, but unfortunately, soon after that, my old feelings began to surface. I loved being a mother but struggled to be a loving wife. I did not understand this; as much as I wanted to be loved and believed I did not receive love growing up, I did not know how to give love at this time. Again, I was not raised on the Godly principles of love and its definition. Also, I did not see true love expressed between my parents. Though I thought I knew what love was, unfortunately, I did not. True love comes from God, and I had not acknowledged His true love for me at this time. If you truly love someone, you will be pure because true love comes from God, and God tells us to remain pure. That is enough for me.

After graduation, my original plan was to attend college; because I wanted a break from school, I decided not to start college at that time and work full time. I was very independent and wanted to make my own money, though the Provider did not want me to work. I tried very hard to be the wife the Provider needed me to be, but I was still unsure how. I wanted to live as a teenager, have fun, and meet new people. I would go out frequently and have the mindset of a single woman and not the mindset of a married woman.

During this time, I met a young man who I begin to really like. I thought he was the true love I had been looking for. How could I be falling for another man, and I was a married woman? How could I believe loving this young man was true love instead of accepting the true love of my husband? Because I did not know the true love of God, I was so confused. I believed God was beginning to convict me. I knew what I was doing was wrong, and I wanted to make things right. I ended the relationship with the guy I was seeing. I wanted to do the right thing and I would tell myself, I was going home to my husband, that I love, and that I would be the wife he needed me to be. However, when I got home, the opposite happened. I could not give true love when I did not know what it was or had it inside of me to give.

I did not know how to love my husband, and I was so confused. I could not understand why I would continue to hurt someone who showed me all the love and affection that I desired. When we do not heal from traumatic experiences in life, we remain broken. The definition of "broken" is damaged or altered. When we are altered physically, mentally, or spiritually, we make poor choices and repeat bad behaviors. If you have not discovered who you are in Christ and what the word of God says about His love for you, you will never know what unconditional love is or how to value and love yourself. The Bible says, "This book of the law shall not depart from your mouth, but you shall meditate on it day and night, so that you may be careful to do according to all that is written in it. For then you will make your way prosperous and then you will have good success" (Joshua 1:8, ESV).

I did not want to continue to hurt him, and I did not want to continue to hurt myself by remaining in a marriage that was not based on true love. Finally, I decided to move out and end the marriage. I had not fully developed a relationship with God, but I began seeking Him and praying to Him. God is a forgiving God, so I was praying for forgiveness. 1 John 1:9 (NIV) says, "if we confess our sins, he is faithful and just and will forgive us of our sins and purify us for our unrighteousness." I did not want to sin against God, so I vowed from that day forward that I would not be unfaithful or commit adultery again. I can honestly say that I kept that vow in the years to come.

Infidelity is Wrong

Infidelity, or adultery, is wrong in the eyes of the Lord. Proverbs says, "But the man who commits adultery is an utter fool, for he destroys himself" (Proverbs 6:32, NLT). When I reflect, I learned the value of doing what is right versus doing what is wrong. But how does someone decide between doing the right thing versus doing the wrong thing? If you meditate on the word of God and gain a proper understanding of His love and how to love others, you should be more compelled to do what is right according to God's word. I must admit it is not always easy doing the right thing, and it was not easy for me.

However, even though I did not have a complete relationship with God, I felt convicted. God placed it in my spirit that what I was doing was not right, and I felt horrible about what I was doing. I no longer had the desire to cause pain or hurt to someone and be displeasing in the eyes of the Lord. Even though I wanted to do the right thing, I was still very broken. I still had the desire to be loved and to love someone truly. However, I never healed from the love lost from the initial experiences of feeling rejected, neglected, and abandoned, and I continued to experience these feelings.

My feelings of brokenness continued to grow. I did not know how to bring myself out of my broken state. I did not know what resources were available to help me cope with what I was experiencing, nor did I know that the main resource I needed to help me cope was the word of God. Since I did not completely know and understand that the word of God was the formal guide or resource I needed, I didn't use the Bible to help me overcome the issues that led to my brokenness.

The word of God is the blueprint of life. The word of God guides and navigates you through life. The word of God molds you into the image of our Heavenly Father. The word of God provides provision, and most importantly, the word of God teaches you about His unconditional love.

CHAPTER 4

BACK ON THE PATHWAY
TO FINDING LOVE

Through many tears, I made the painful decision to end my marriage and the relationship I had outside of my marriage. I did not want to continue to hurt anyone else, including myself. Meditating and reading His word became a daily habit, and I would look up scriptures that applied to specific issues in my life. This helped me learn about His love, self-love, and how to love others.

Since I left my husband and filed for divorce, I was now at a point in my life where I was raising two small children alone. It was a struggle. We lived in a one-bedroom apartment, and I did not have a car. I received a minimum of two hundred dollars in child support every two weeks for two small children, was on food stamps and worked part-time. Because of all the guilt, I felt for cheating on my first husband, I did not fight during the divorce and just accepted the minimal amount of child support.

It was a struggle being on my own for the first time, raising two small children, paying rent, and not having a car. However, I was very independent and determined to make things happen to support my boys. Even during my marriage, I always wanted to work and have my own income.

Even though most of the time I felt unloved and unworthy, I am grateful to have the desire in me to want more for myself professionally and be able to provide for my children. I believe God instilled in me the desire to always want to improve and better myself professionally. Though going to college was not the right decision during that time, I always wanted to be in the medical field, so I decided to attend a six-month medical assistant program. This added to my daily struggle to attend school, work part-time, and raise two small children. Nevertheless, I was determined to succeed, and I did.

True love vs lust

Months after my divorce, I reconnected with the young man I thought I was in love with when I was married. I would call him the Hustler because he was a local street hustler. He was not a good provider like my first husband. However, he always came through when I needed him the most. Since he did not have a 9 to 5 job, he would keep the boys when I was in school or when I had to work.

In the beginning, the Hustler and I had fun together. We were the same age and in love, or so I thought, but I recognized it was mainly lust. No one made me feel the way he did. We would have arguments and then have make-up sex. After having sex, I would forget the argument and be in love all over again. We had our challenges, but overall I was happy that I finally "thought" I had someone in my life I was in love with and who truly loved me.

We were together for five years before we grew apart. He was in and out of jail, and I began to desire more for myself. I decided it was time to attend college and go to nursing school. After making that decision, my life became hectic since I went to school during the week and worked long hours on the weekend. The Hustler and I were still together, but our relationship was definitely different from how it was in the beginning. While sex kept us together, that came to an end.

I wish I had loved myself enough not to get involved in relationships that were not right from the beginning, but for years, I learned the hard way. At the time, if I knew the word of God and what his word said about true love and self-worth, I would have avoided many unnecessary and painful mistakes. With God's love and guidance, I eventually learned to love myself. However, I had to endure several more bad relationships before I got to that point.

After the Hustler and I split up, my main priorities were work, nursing school, and raising the boys. At this point, I also tried to help my mother and father overcome their addictions. However, each attempt failed with both. The disappointment that I continue to endure just added to my brokenness. I would continue to cry while reminiscing on the pain and heartache I endured from my parents and past relationships and the pain I caused.

I was very sad and depressed and still craved love and affection. Oh, but the love of God. At the time, I did not know how much God loved me. Later, I realized that I was not alone because He was always by my side. God comforted me during those times and brought me out of my sadness. "Praise be to the God and Father of our Lord Jesus Christ, the Father of Compassion, and the God of all comfort" (2 Corinthians 1:3, NIV). "He heals the brokenhearted and binds up their wounds" (Psalm 147:3, NIV).

.

CHAPTER 5

PATHWAY OF DEPRESSION

It was normal for me to date for a short period of time without making any serious commitments at the time. I continued to struggle in relationships, but I was doing well in other areas of my life. I was making progress in my nursing career; I completed my prerequisite nursing courses at a Community College and finished with a 3.8 GPA. After completing my courses, I was accepted and transferred to a nursing program at a very prestigious college.

I was doing well academically, but my continued desire for love resurfaced. I met a young man who wasn't my ideal man. Typically, I am attracted to tall, dark-skinned men, but this young man was the opposite: he was short and light-browned skinned. In my opinion, he did not have much going for himself except that he worked a 9-to-5 job. I was so in love with the idea of being in love that I made myself see the potential in this young man, and I liked that he was interested in me. This idea caused me to make myself available for him and lose focus on my nursing goals. I was more focused on trying to please him so that he would love me like I felt I deserved to be loved.

Depression Begins

As much as I tried to make this relationship with the young man work, it eventually failed. I made myself available to him, but he eventually stopped calling or coming around. I could not understand why he did not love me as I thought he should. I settled for him and made myself available for him. The way he treated me just added to my unresolved issues of unworthiness and rejection, which led to me becoming more depressed.

In my depressed state, I would listen to sad love songs and cry off and on day and night. I even lost weight during this time because I had no desire to eat. What made matters worse was that I lost focus and failed nursing school. God had already shown me mercy when I passed a class I should have failed. My teacher gave me a passing grade on my last test, which allowed me to pass the class. I was saved because "through the Lord's mercies we are not consumed, because his compassions fail not" (Lamentations 3:22, NKJV). God showed me mercy for one class, and you would think I would have been more grateful.

Unfortunately, I was not, and because I allowed my desire to love a man who did not love me to take priority, I ended up flunking out of nursing school. How did I become this way after only dating this young man for six months?

How could I allow myself to lose focus and flunk out of nursing school, especially when I had worked hard to get to where I was? Why was my love for people greater than my love for myself? All these internal questions just added to the depression. I was never suicidal, but I had no desire to keep moving forward to do anything when I felt this way.

Causes of Depression and Deliverance

Depression can be caused by alterations in your brain, genetics, stressful life situations, or medical conditions. Unfortunately, my feelings of depression were brought on by repeated cycles of rejection and heartache. Symptoms of depression can range from mild to moderate and sometimes require medical attention. The symptoms I experienced were sadness, loss of appetite, loss of energy, and loss of interest in activities. I did not think I needed help, nor did I know how to help myself.

I am so grateful for God's mercy in my life. He gave me the strength to overcome my moments of depression. God helped me get out of my depression by directing my love and attention back to the two people who loved me, and I loved them. Psalm declares, "I waited patiently for the Lord to help me, and he turned to me and heard my cry. He lifted me out of the pit of despair, out of the mud and the mire. He set my feet on solid ground and steadied me as I walked along. He has given me a new song to sing, a hymn of praise to our God. Many will see what he has done and be amazed. They will put their trust in the Lord" (Psalm 40:1-3, NLT).

God's grace and mercy freed me from my depressed state and allowed me to regain focused on the important things in my life. When I regained focus, I enrolled back in community college to take a few more classes. After that, I applied to another prestigious nursing school and was accepted into the nursing program.

Throughout the years, my struggle to be loved resulted in many failed relationships. However, my strong desire to want more professionally proved to be beneficial. One thing is for sure: I did love myself enough to want to provide a better life for my children. As their mother, it was just in me to provide them with all my love and affection and protect them the best way I knew how. I thought the love and protection I provided for my children were enough to shield them from the rejections, neglect, and heartaches I had experienced. As much as I tried to protect them from what I experienced, my desire to be loved led to my brokenness, exposing them to what I thought I was protecting them from.

I exposed my children to the individuals that led to my feelings of brokenness and unloved. How can one truly love another when they don't love themselves? Unconditional love allows you to love yourself first and then give that same love to someone else. God's love is unconditional.

By meditating on His word, you discover God's, unconditional love. After learning His love, He teaches you how to love yourself. Once you love yourself, you will know your true worth, develop expectations for love, and learn how to love others.

.

CHAPTER 6

PATHWAY OF DESTRUCTION

At that point in my life, I was a woman who had been divorced, experienced two other bad relationships, and suffered a minor setback when I flunked out of nursing school. I was alone and did not have friends or family to confide in for support. Nor were my parents in a mental state to support me emotionally or physically. I began to draw closer to God. I began praying more and reading my Bible. Even though I began praying more, I still did not know the full extent of His true and unconditional love.

At this time, I worked on weekends, went to school during the day, and focused on raising my boys. I thought my life would be busy enough, and I would not be focused on wanting to be in another relationship; sadly, I was wrong. I continued to have the overwhelming desire to be in a loving relationship. I felt that was all I needed to complete myself. Instead of remaining focused on school, work, and my boys, I began going out with friends to meet people. And then it happened—my next pathway of destruction began.

Meeting in the Club

With a second opportunity to return to nursing school and receive my degree, one would have thought I would have taken this opportunity more seriously. Instead, my desire for love wanted me to hang out with people I knew and go out to clubs.

One night I went out to the club and met a young man whom I will call the Controller. He was tall, handsome, and had light brown eyes. He also had a white Corvette at the time. He called me, and we had one conversation on the phone. However, for whatever reason at the time, the relationship did not go any further. There was a reason I had no interest in this young man then, and I should have kept that in the back of my mind.

About two months later, I met the Controller again at a nightclub. Because of my strong desire to be in a relationship, I thought that it was fate that we reconnected. I did not remember why I did not connect with him the first time. However, it did not matter. I connected with him again, and I was not going to let him get away. I had been praying to God for a man, and I thought he was my answered prayer from God. Unfortunately, the devil knows the areas we are weak in and would place things or people in our path to tempt us in those areas. When we do not have a true relationship with God, we fall for those temptations that will hold us back from God's promises. As I later learned, the Controller was not an answered prayer from GOD.

When I met the Controller for the second time, he lived with his parents and did not have the Corvette anymore due to financial difficulties. He shared with me the financial situation was temporary, and he was working on improving his situation. Regardless of his financial difficulties, he treated me very well in the beginning. He would come over to my apartment and cook for me. He would clean my home if needed. He started off having a good relationship with my boys. I have discovered that sometimes individuals will go out of their way to show you good things while using these efforts to cover up the truth. With all the good things the Controller showed me, something in my spirit warned me that something was just not right with this man. Unfortunately, because of my desire for love, I allowed all those temporary good things to cover up the warning signs.

With my first marriage, I believe God was working through the preacher when he informed us that something was wrong with the relationship and we were not ready for marriage, but I did not listen. This time and many times after, the Holy Spirit within me would forewarn me of negative situations. "Do you not know that you are the temple of God, and that Spirit of God dwells in you" (1 Cor 3:16, ESV). The Holy Spirit would speak to us when our choices and decisions did not align with the word of God. I did not always listen to my inner spirit, and because I did not listen, I continued to make bad decisions about the men I chose to be in a relationship with.

Controlling Behavior Begins

There is a reason why I named this man the Controller.

He came into my life, leading me to believe he was a great man, only to disillusion me and begin taking control of my life. First, he did not want me to hang out with my few friends. Next, he convinced me to allow him to move in with me. When he moved in with me, he replaced all my furniture with his. So, I stored my furniture at his parent's home; I never retrieved or saw my furniture again.

Before we moved in together, I knew he drank alcohol sociably. However, after we moved in together, I learned he drank often, and drinking led to his aggressive and controlling behavior. When he was under the influence of alcohol, he would start arguments that would lead to physical fights. The Controller revealed to me about a night he and his father had been drinking. He became so angry with his father and knocked him out. He also revealed to me about a time he got into a fight with someone at a night club. Because of this incident, he was paying restitution to this man.

Once we moved in together, his aggressive and controlling behavior quickly manifested. He began trying to isolate me from my family and the few friends I had. He then started to control how I dressed; he wanted me to wear long dresses, nothing short or too revealing. Being with the Controller led me to a very dark and negative place and people began to observe a change in my behavior.

My coworker at work noticed the negative impact this relationship had on me. One day my co-worker stated that since I have been in a relationship with the controller, my behavior had changed. She described how my morale seemed low and my physical appearance had changed for the worse. She mentioned how I was always shopping and going to the hair salon. However, that changed, and she noticed.

As if trying to change and control me wasn't enough, he tried to change and control the relationship I had with my boys. The most disturbing issue that developed over time was that he became jealous of my relationship with my boys. He demonstrated this by speaking negatively to my boys, particularly my oldest son. For whatever reason, the Controller acted as if he had a personal vendetta against my oldest son. I did not understand because he was only a child. I tried to make the best of this situation and cover up all the things that were surfacing.

The Abuse Begins

The abuse began verbally; he would get upset and yell about the smallest things. It then escalated from verbal to physical; his yelling would lead to pushing and shoving me around. Most of the verbal and physical abuse occurred after he had been drinking.

The Controller would often go out and drink with his friends. While he was out drinking with his friends, he would call home several times to find something to come home and argue about. We would always argue and fight when he came home after being out drinking with his friends. Even though we would physically fight, he never punched me with his fist. However, he would drag me around or slap me.

His behavior occurred early in the relationship. I should

have been smart enough to end this relationship as soon as the negative behaviors began to manifest. However, I wanted to be in a loving relationship. My desire for love was so strong that I proceeded to marry the Controller when I should not have. Two weeks before we got married, we fought. The way he shoved me, I ended up with a broken finger. I should have ended the relationship, but I did not.

Looking back, I don't know why I proceeded to marry him after that, but I believe the reason is that I felt trapped. I said I would never be with an abusive man after seeing my father abuse my mother, but here I was in an abusive relationship, and I didn't know how to get out of it. Like most individuals in abusive relationships, we see abuse as a form of love. He always apologized after the fights and went out of his way to make things better. But it was just a repeated cycle that kept getting worse. We eloped and got married in Las Vegas. In total, we were together for three years: 1.5 years before marriage and 1.5 years after marriage. Being married to the Controller was like an up-and-down roller coaster ride that I did not know how to stop so that I could get off.

The Controller was aggressive and controlling and had an anger management problem. Because he did not know how to control his anger, he could not keep a job for an extended period. He would constantly disagree, get angry with his supervisors, and then get fired or laid off, so he was often in between jobs. During this time, his drinking worsened, and he was always angry and aggressive. Anything would set him off, and he would become angry for no apparent reason. I remember a time when he allowed himself to become so angry for nothing that he took out the dresser drawer, smashed it against the dresser, and broke it. He then dragged me from my bedroom to the bathroom tub and attempted to drown me.

The police were called out, and I was able to get my belongings and leave. My father lived down the street then, and the boys and I moved in with him. My father was trying to get his life together but was failing miserably. As much as I did not want to move in with my father, I had nowhere else to go. Moving back with my father ignited all the abandonment and neglect issues I experienced as a young child because my father still had drug and alcohol problems. However, for the moment, being with my father was better than being with the Controller.

The Controller knew where my father lived. One morning, when I was about to leave for school, I found two tires missing from my car. I was devasted and should have called the police. However, I did not because I had a test that morning and was determined to get to class. I had to ride the bus, which made me late for class. On the way to school, I called my teacher and explained what was happening. God's grace and love for me were shown by my teacher's understanding and allowing me to proceed with my test. With all that I went through that morning, I passed my test. The Bible says, "The righteous person may have many troubles, but the Lord delivers him from all" (Psalm 34:19, NIV). I was upset about what the Controller did. However, I was naive and did not proceed in filing a police report.

I could not endure living with my father for such a long

time. Living with him was a constant reminder of how my brokenness began. After a couple of months of living with my father, my boys and I moved into another apartment. The Controller did not know where I lived, but he would constantly pop up at my job asking for my forgiveness. And, of course, I took him back.

The Controller convinced me that he loved me and was going to change. After we reconciled, I allowed him to move back in with me. Before he moved back, I had a sit-down conversation with my boys to explain why I accepted him. Their little faces showed me their disapproval. Why was my desire to be loved greater than protecting and loving my children at that time? This is the same question that I would ask about my parents. Why was their love greater for their addictions than it was for me? The Bible teaches us that for us to give love, we must first know and understand the love of God. 1 John says, "And as we live in God, our love grows more perfect. We love each other because he loved us first" (1 John 4:17-19, NLT). My parents and I did not grow up knowing the love of God and how his love guided us in making wise decisions.

Finally Listening

It was not long before his abusive behavior began again. God began to forewarn me of what could happen if I continued being with the Controller. I had three identical dreams. I dreamt that my oldest son had lost consciousness and fallen to the ground. It was like he was in a fight and got knocked out. I did not know the significance of the dream until one night when it almost became a reality. On Martin

Luther King Day, the Controller was out drinking with his friends, and of course, he called me to start an argument before he came home. I laid back down after the phone call. Immediately after I laid down, the Holy Spirit in me told me to get up and quickly get my children and get out of that apartment. This was one of the times I listened to the Holy Spirit within me.

I left the apartment and parked across the street. I did not know what to do or where to go. I waited there until I decided what to do. My father lost his apartment, so we could not go back to his place. I thought about my mother, but I would hear from her every so often. Sometimes she would reside in this run-down apartment building, and I would go and visit her at times. I did not have anyone else to turn to, so I took my chances and went to where my mother lived. It was by God's grace that she was there. God knew I needed guidance at this time, and my mother was there for me for once. I got us a hotel for the night and decided to go down to the courthouse and file for a protective order the following day.

When I arrived at the courthouse to file a protective order, the lady who assisted me was not convinced that I presented enough evidence to file a protective order against the Controller. She was not convinced because I had never filed a police report against him for domestic violence. The one time I did call the police, I did not file a report. The police allowed him to leave so I could retrieve my belongings.

The lady began to consider my situation after my oldest

son revealed a situation he experienced with the Controller one week before this incident. The Controller forced my oldest son to ride with him. He tormented and chastised my son. My son revealed that he was yelling at him, cursing him out, and grabbing him by his shirt. The Controller left scratches on my son's neck and chest.

I was devastated. I felt like the worst mother ever. My son was afraid to tell me because the Controller threatened him. Like most abusers, they instill fear in victims so they will not report the abuse. However, learning about what happened to my son, was still not enough evidence to support filing a protective order against the Controller?

We were still at the courthouse when my inner spirit told me to call my apartment complex to check on things. The people in the leasing office were very concerned about me. That night, the Controller came to the apartment and caused a lot of commotion. The apartment was destroyed. There was glass everywhere because he broke out the apartment's front window. All his belongings were removed, but he destroyed all my belongings. He broke all the remaining items and furniture I had left. He bleached all the scrubs I wore for my clinical at school. He also took my boys' electronic game systems. Because we were not there when he arrived to endure his abusive behavior, he showed his abusive behavior by destroying the apartment. The lady at the courthouse was now convinced that I had enough evidence to file a protective order against the Controller.

Thank God my mother was still supporting me because I was an emotional wreck. We left the courthouse and proceeded to my apartment. I had the police meet me there to file a report. The window was boarded up when we arrived, and he left me with nothing. But God's love for me allowed me to leave that night with our lives. I can't even begin to imagine what would have occurred if I had stayed that night. God showed me what would have happened in my three identical dreams. If I had stayed, the Controller would have come home and hurt my son. I would have never forgiven myself if this had occurred. But oh, the grace of God. His love for us rescued us from the hands of our enemy.

Forced to move and move on

Since the Controller was not on the lease and he destroyed the property, the manager in the leasing office informed me that I had to move. The manager allowed me to get out of my lease without it going against me as a broken lease. I had thirty days to move out. Through God's grace, I was able to move into the apartments across the street. The apartments were much nicer but much smaller. It did not really matter because I did not have any furniture. The Controller destroyed everything me and the boys had, except my bed. It was difficult to adjust from living in a larger, fully furnished apartment to a smaller one with minimal furniture.

Going through the abuse and losing everything we had was depressing for my boys and me. My boys were also disappointed because the Controller had taken both video game systems. My oldest asked me if he could pack up those games the night we left. I told him no because we did not have time for that. All I wanted us to do was get out of there before he returned. This made me feel worse about the situation because I should have allowed him to pack up their game systems.

Even though things appeared very dismal and sad, God continued to show me His love and grace. Before I graduated from nursing school, I worked the night shift. A nurse on the unit I worked on was informed about what I was going through with the Controller. At first, I was upset that my friend discussed what I was going through with her, but she was a blessing in disguise. As a woman of God, she informed me that God put it in her spirit to help me. The lady was very gracious by offering to assist me in buying some furniture. She allowed me to pay her back in installments. I purchased a sofa bed, two end tables, and a dinette set.

Words cannot express the gratitude I felt during this time. God made a way for my children and me when I did not foresee a way out. He allowed me to move into a nicer apartment in a short amount of time without the eviction damaging my rental history. God allowed my mother to support me when I needed her the most. She did not remain with me for a long time, but I was very grateful for the time she was there. God placed someone in my life to assist me in my time of need. And what mattered the most was that I could replace my sons' electronic game systems. Once again, the Lord was showing me how much He loved me. "God saw the trouble I was in, his love never fails. God rescued me from my enemies, his love never fails" (See Psalm 136:23-24, CEV).

Coping with Abuse

Wikipedia defines domestic abuse as "any form of abusive behavior by one or both partners in an intimate relationship, such as marriage, cohabitation, family, dating, or even friendship." Abusive behaviors can result in several forms of abuse; such as, physical abuse, domestic violence/abuse, sexual abuse, emotional abuse or financial abulse, the . Domestic abuse should in no way be considered love. When I observed my father physically abusing my mother, I did not think he loved her, and I swore I would never be involved with someone physically violent. In my desire to be loved, I found myself with a person I swore I would never be with.

Considering that I was exposed to physical abuse as a child, I questioned why I did not recognize the signs. However, I was a child when I first witnessed physical abuse, and I did not know what signs to look for. In the beginning, the Controller showed signs of controlling behavior, such as wanting to move in and live together too soon, constantly discussing his violent behaviors towards others in his past, and possessiveness. In time, those signs escalated, and other abusive behaviors manifested.

When things don't seem right in the beginning, they typically are not right and will not be right in the end. We should be alert to these behaviors and address them before they manifest into a situation that results in someone being battered, abused, and unable to get out of the situation. It is very important to recognize abuse and avoid relationships with abusive people. Being in an abusive relationship is very unfortunate and challenging. Seeking counsel and meditating on God's word will help you overcome. "From oppression and violence he redeems their life, and precious is their blood in his sight" (Psalm 72:14, NIV).

CHAPTPER 7

MOVING ON

Being married to the Controller had an emotional, physical, and financial impact on me and the boys. I was able to replace some of the material things that we had lost, but nothing could replace the emotional impact of going through such an experience. Though I was broken and looking for love, I thought I was shielding my boys from experiencing what I felt. In actuality, I was doing the exact opposite, putting them in harm's way.

They witnessed the arguments and the physical encounters I endured with the Controller. I did not think my decisions at the time would negatively impact my children, but they did. After the encounter with the Controller, though my youngest son was quiet and did not always show his emotions, I knew he was fearful of the Controller.

My oldest became very angry after the encounter with

the Controller, but who could blame him for feeling the way he was feeling? I can't imagine how traumatizing it was as a child to be tortured by an abusive adult. I was very concerned about the behaviors I began to observe in my children, which led us to seek family counseling.

Family Counseling

I loved my boys. I used to have deep conversations with them. I did not want them to make the same mistakes I made in the past or my current mistakes. I did not want them to feel as if I did not love them. To ensure that this situation did not leave us with negative emotional behaviors, I decided we should seek family counseling..

We went to a Christian family counselor, but the counseling session was not positive. The counselor did not provide a therapeutic environment for me to open up to him. However, we did discuss a little of my past and the situation we just encountered with the Controller. The most I took away from the session was when my oldest son said he did not trust me. He believed that I would allow the Controller back into our lives. Hearing that broke me down. If I did not realize it before, I realized then how my decisions in relationships impacted my children. After an hour or more in the counseling session, the only advice the counselor gave was that he believed the boys were going to be just fine. He was more concerned with me and said that I should continue with individual counseling. However, I decided not to continue counseling.

First, I did not feel a connection with the counselor. Second, he dismissed my children's behaviors and did not address my son's comment that he no longer trusted me. He should have suggested that we need family counseling to rebuild lost trust and correct the behaviors. I just stopped going. Why did I stop going? It was evident I was broken and needed healing. Looking back, I should have searched for another counselor with whom we had a better connection to assist in my healing process and to rebuild the broken bond between my children and me. My children and I eventually healed and regained each other's trust. However, this trust was established many years later. If I had continued the family counseling initially, we would have healed sooner.

Life after the Protective Order

After the protective order was filed, I had to go to a hearing for the protective order to become legally binding. I was very nervous, and I did not know what to expect. It was now March, and I had not seen the Controller since January. But thank God, my mother was there to help support me through this time. I went to look for her the night before the hearing, and through God's amazing grace, I found her. She stayed with me overnight and went to the hearing with me the next day.

After the hearing, the protective order became legally binding. The protective order was in place for two years, which made me relieved and thankful. Another blessing in disguise was that his friend was his lawyer at the hearing and convinced him to file for divorce. He filed for divorce in February, and the divorce was finalized in March. I was thankful I did not have to pay for the divorce. The protective order and my divorce were put in place simultaneously, which meant my life with the Controller was officially over, and I was elated about that fact.

After the traumatic experience with the Controller, I had two months before I graduated from nursing school. After failing nursing school once before, I was determined to succeed and graduate this time, and I was finally going to graduate in May. I worked too hard to get to this point in my life, and I was not going to let anything hinder me from graduating from nursing school. It was difficult, but I worked it out the best way I could as the boys and I tried to put our lives back together. I was not going to let what happened with the Controller stop me from graduating.

To help me get through my struggles at that time, I was seeking God. "God is our refuge and strength, a very present help in trouble" (Psalm 46:1, ESV). I was praying and reading my Bible more; however, unfortunately, I was not getting a true understanding of God's love and his word. If I did, I would have been praying for his love and the purpose he had for my life. Instead, I prayed for love and what I thought was best for my life.

Today, I get upset with myself when I look at how I failed to realize the love I was seeking, which he was providing. Why was I not listening and acknowledging the things He was showing me through the Holy Spirit within me? Why was I not allowing myself to heal emotionally and be made whole? God had just rescued the boys and me from the Controller, and I still wanted to be in a loving relationship with a physical being.

Unfortunately, the overwhelming desire to be in a loving relationship was still upon me, and I could not understand why. Therefore, I should have continued counseling. I would have been working through my issues instead of continuing to fuel these destructive desires. This desire was like an addiction that I just could not overcome. I just came out of another bad relationship and was ready to get involved in another one. The outcome of this last relationship could have ended worse than it did.

So why would I have the continued desire to get involved in another relationship? I had not dealt with or healed from this last relationship or all the past hurts and pains I had experienced over the years. Paula White Cain says, "You cannot overcome your condition until you know your position. You really don't know who you are until you discover it through your relationship with God through His Son, Jesus Christ. Knowing your position in Christ Jesus gives you the power to overcome any condition related to your past."

During that time, my inner spirit was speaking to me to find and contact my friend, whom I stopped associating with when I was with the Controller. I did not act on these feelings at first. I did not have her number, but I did know where her grandmother lived. I went to her grandmother's house and left my number for her to call. She did, and we became reacquainted. She shared with me that she was dating someone at the time. He had a friend she thought was very nice, and she wanted me to meet him. I was initially reluctant because I needed to heal from my last relationship. However, I still had the desire to be in a loving relationship. So, after a few "no, I don't want to meet him" responses, I decided to meet him. This blind date resulted in another bad relationship that lasted eleven years.

There are two things I regret that would have assisted me in overcoming these destructive desires sooner rather than later. The first is that, even though I was reading the word of God, I was not applying the word of God to heal from my brokenness. The desire to be in a loving relationship was a stronghold over me. If I had applied the word of God to my life sooner rather than later, I would not have continued down the destructive path I was on.

I discovered that even though I did not have a physical person to turn to for guidance and support, the Word of God was always available to me. Psalm 91:14–16 (ESV) states, "Because he holds fast to me in love, I will deliver him: I will protect him because he knows my name. When he calls me, I will answer him; I will be with him in trouble; I will rescue him and honor him. With long life I will satisfy him and show him my salvation".

If I had read the word for guidance, I would have applied his word to the issues of my life. I should have been on the pathway to discovering his unconditional love. God's word on love and self-worth is reflected in Isaiah 43:4 (ESV) "you are precious in my eyes, and honored, and I love you." God's word helps us overcome strongholds because "he gives power to the weak and strength to the powerless" (Isaiah 40:29, NLT).

The second thing I regret is not continuing counseling.

Counseling would have assisted me with identifying and correcting behaviors that continued to make me feel broken. According to "Benefits and Options for Therapy" by Sara Lindberg on healthline.com, the benefits of counseling are:

1. Helps improve communication skills
2. Helps you feel empowered
3. Empowers you to develop fresh insights about your life
4. Learn how to make healthier choices
5. Develop coping strategies to manage distress
6. Evaluate and treat behavioral problems
7. Individual coping strategies
8. Address relationship issues within the context of the family system

I know I would have overcome my issues by applying the word of God to my life and continuing therapy. If I had done this at this time, I would not have continued to make bad decisions in relationships, and I would have come to love myself and discover my worth.

CHAPTER 8

FROM ONE PATHWAY OF DESTRUCTION TO ANOTHER

I wish I could say, after all I have encountered, that I would have known better and made better decisions when it came to my pathway of love. But I did not make better decisions beyond this point, and my destructive path continued. Within months, I went from one bad relationship to another.

It had been three months since the traumatic experience with the Controller and adjusting to our new life. My boys and I were dealing with the trauma we endured with the Controller in our way. My youngest was a little withdrawn and began gaining a lot of weight, and my oldest son was always angry. I kept open communication with them to allow them to express and work through their feelings. I also wanted to build our relationship and allow them to feel as if they could trust me again, no matter what.

I was trying to be the best mother I could be for them. However, I was still very broken and had not healed from all the hurt I had experienced in my previous relationships. Even with the desire to support and guide my children and knowing how broken I am, I still believe that finding someone else will help me heal from my brokenness. So there I was again, about to continue down the wrong pathway.

As I mentioned before, I had previously gone on a blind date that my friend convinced me to do; however, she did not have to do much convincing. Even though I was happy because I was graduating from nursing school, that still did not take away my desire to be loved. I will call the young man I met on the blind date the Charmer. He was exactly what his name represented: charm and charisma. He displayed many positive characteristics that attracted me to him. He was handsome, dark-skinned, and dressed well. I noticed that he was very considerate and thoughtful and had a large family. I like that he had a big family and was a family man, considering I was the only child and was not very close to many of my other relatives.

Since he was very friendly and outgoing, we always enjoyed ourselves when we attended social events. The Charmer and I had fun together. I had the best birthdays when I was with the Charmer. I must admit that he brought joy and happiness into my life. Unfortunately, the joy was accompanied by many heartaches and pains.

The Cheating Begins

The Charmer charmed me off my feet. He moved in with me three months after we met. Who does this? Who gets involved so quickly in another relationship after experiencing what I had experienced with the Controller. My desire to be in a relationship and loved superseded my listening to my inner spirit, which told me I was moving too fast. It felt like love, but what I later experienced in this relationship was far from love.

We did not date long enough to really get to know each other. I discovered a lot of his past after we moved in together. For example, I discovered he had a criminal past and had never been in a monogamous relationship. He informed me that he often prayed during the last time he was incarcerated. He wrote a letter to God, asking for forgiveness and for Him to deliver him from the desire to date multiple women at one time. He charmed me into believing I was the woman he could be in a monogamous relationship with. However, five months into the relationship, I discovered he cheated.

When I found out he cheated, I was furious and was going to throw him out of my apartment. He pleaded for my forgiveness, stating he would never cheat again or do anything to hurt me. Of course, I forgave him. I wanted so much to be loved by someone. When I think back, I wonder, "Why was my desire for love so strong that I allowed myself to get involved with men who claimed to love me but did not?" My strong desire to be loved led me to a place that kept me in a broken state. Because I have not healed from my brokenness, I continued down this destructive pathway, allowing others to hurt me. I allowed others to treat me the way they did because I did not love myself or value myself the way I deserved to be loved and valued.

I wish I could say that the Charmer became loyal to me and never cheated on me again after the first cheating episode, but that is far from the truth. He continued to cheat with random women. My inner spirit would speak to me, or I would have dreams warning me when something was wrong. I used to work the night shift. However, I began to have this overall feeling that I needed to find a day-shift position as a nurse. At first, I thought that I needed to change shifts to be at home more with the boys. However, I later discovered that working nights allowed the Charmer to be free and have time to cheat, so I eventually found a dayshift job. I wish I could say that my working the day shift prevented the Charmer from cheating, but again, I was wrong. He would cheat, I would find out, break up with him, forgive him, and then he would cheat again. This was a repeated cycle for eleven years.

Picture Perfect vs the Fast Life

There were two sides to the Charmer. There was the side that wanted the picture-perfect family life; he genuinely cared for my boys. From the beginning, he worked to build a positive relationship with them, providing for them and supporting them in all their extracurricular activities. We were always together as a family at family gatherings and social events. Looking at us from the outside, we looked like a perfect family. But behind closed doors, we were far from the picture-perfect family. No one knew the heartaches I experienced.

Then there was his other side, the side that was addicted to what I call the "fast life." The Charmer's fast life included how he was in his previous life. He involved himself in activities that were not lawful, associated himself with the wrong individuals, and dated multiple women at a time. The Charmer was very good at keeping his picture-perfect family life separate from his fast life. I wish I could say that his desire for the picture-perfect family life was greater than his desire for the fast life, but unfortunately, it was not.

Why did I allow myself to continue to accept the Charmer's behavior? As I look back, I realize the importance of reading God's word and applying it to every aspect of your life. I did not know how to get out of this relationship because I felt stuck. One reason is that I did not love myself enough to demand the respect and love I deserved, so I just accepted his behavior. Secondly, he developed a great bond with my boys, and I did not want to remove him from their lives. My boys loved him, and he loved them. My boys only saw the loving side of him. Since I protected them, they had no clue about the heartache and pain I was experiencing.

As the picture-perfect family, we grew financially. I had a career as a nurse; we started several businesses and had rental properties. On the other hand, he also grew more addicted to the fast life. He continued to engage in activities that were not lawful, and he cheated more frequently. We were successful and growing in so many ways that he could have avoided the fast life. However, I guess his desire for the fast life were just as strong for him as being in a loving relationship was for me. These strong desires did not lead us to make the right decisions for our lives.

I wish I could say that things were getting better. Unfortunately, things went from bad to worse. Not only was I dealing with the Charmer's infidelity, but I was also dealing with some negative behaviors from my oldest son. He was a typical rebellious, angry teenager and crazy about girls. I know most of his anger developed from what happened with the Controller. However, as his mother, I was not going to allow him to be out of control and do what he wanted to do. My boys had so much potential, and I tried hard not to make decisions that would not allow them to become the best they could be.

How can I expect my boys to avoid the mistakes I made when they witnessed so many of my mistakes? I tried to be the best mother I could be for them. I wanted so much for them; I did not want them to feel unloved or encounter all I had experienced over the years. I was always very open and transparent with my boys. We talked all the time about avoiding the wrong crowd, drugs, and teenage parenting. And then it happened: My 16-year-old son informed me that he was about to become a father.

Here I go again. How could someone I love so much cause me such heartache and pain? When my son informed me of this, it was like a knife going straight through my heart. This pain led me into a deep depression for several days. I could not get out of bed, and I cried non-stop. I was calling out to God, asking, why did this happen? What did I do wrong?

Am I not a good mother? I cried out to God to take the pain away and help me find the strength to deal with the situation.

My husband was there but did not know how to support me through this. Oh, but the love of God, I was encouraged by the scripture that says, "And he said, O man greatly loved, fear not, peace be with you; be strong and of good courage. And as he spoke to me, I was strengthened and said, Let my lord speak, for you have strengthened me" (Daniel 10:19, ESV). God's love for me gave me the strength to overcome the pain and depression I was experiencing. His love for me allowed me to understand it was nothing I did wrong. God's love for me allowed me to forgive myself and not be angry with my son. God's love for me showed me how to continue to support my son through this time. I loved my son and was going to be there for him and his child. My grandson was born and quickly became the source of great joy in our lives. Becoming grandparents became a part of our picture-perfect family. However, it was not enough for the Charmer to remain a devoted family man.

From the outside looking in, we continued to look like the picture-perfect family, and we were now loving grandparents. My son got accepted at a prestigious college on a track scholarship. As grandparents, we were preparing to care for my grandson while my son was away at college. This was a good time for us as a family; however, that did not stop the negative things the Charmer was involved in, nor did it stop his cheating.

Even though we were married and looked like the

picture-perfect family, there were many times I felt very alone, unloved, and depressed. I was hurting and could not understand why he kept cheating on me. What was wrong with me? Why did he not love me enough to be faithful to me? No one knew what I was feeling, but these feelings kept building up and adding to all the heartaches and pains I had experienced that had led to my brokenness.

Looking at me from the outside, you would not have known the pain I was experiencing internally. I did not want to continue going through this with the Charmer. At this time, I would constantly pray and seek God's guidance. I began to pray morning, noon, and night. I needed God more than ever. I wanted to leave and divorce him. As I prayed, the Holy Spirit would begin to speak to me and say, "be still and know that I am God" (Psalm 46:10, NIV). And then it happened—another major turning point in my life that again made me feel abandoned. The Charmer was arrested for his involvement in unlawful activity. There was nothing that prepared me for what I was about to endure. However, God's love for me gave me the strength to face the challenges ahead.

When you continue to put Band-Aids over large wounds, it is just a cover, and the wounds do not heal properly. Since I did not take the time to heal between each relationship, I did not allow myself to heal completely. Therefore, my brokenness continued to grow and worsened over time. That is why I made the same repeated mistakes with each relationship. I should have turned to God's word to heal me from my brokenness, as Psalms says, "He heals up the brokenhearted and binds up their wounds" (Psalm

147:3, NKJV).

CHAPTER 9

THE PATHWAY OF DESTRUCTION ENDS

After years of dealing with the Charmer's infidelity, I am now about to deal with the negative consequences of his addiction to the fast life. The Charmer's illegal activities eventually caught up with him, and he was arrested. Even though I was not involved in what he was doing, his actions affected me emotionally, physically, and financially. I have been through so much over the years; this situation was just an added layer to my brokenness.

I did not have a support system to discuss my issues with the Charmer; I internalized all my feelings. When he was arrested, it was broadcast on the evening news. One of my co-workers saw this and informed all my co-workers at my job. I was humiliated, embarrassed, and ashamed by this. My co-workers, who thought I had a picture-perfect life, could now see how broken I was and the issues I had in my marriage. To the coworkers I was close to, I now had to be open and discuss all that I was going through. A few of them supported me through this; however, many continued gossiping about me. I was ashamed, but I continued praying and held my head high. I did not do anything wrong, and I knew God had me covered and would guide me through this circumstance.

The Trial Begins

During this time, the Charmer was in jail awaiting trial. I was loyal and supportive and remained by his side. Even though I was by his side, this was a very difficult time financially and emotionally for me. Financially, I was responsible for paying the attorney's fees, maintaining my household bills, operating our businesses, and managing the rental properties. In addition, to meet all my financial obligations, I had to continue working full-time.

Externally, I had to appear strong, but internally, I was an emotional wreck. Internally, I was stressed out by the fact that everyone now knew what I was going through, including my children. To add to my stress, there was the risk of me being implicated in the Charmer's illegal activities. I was not involved in what he was doing and thank God I was not implicated because I could have lost so much more, including my nursing license, which I worked so hard for.

In addition to everything else, the attorney was preparing me to take the witness stand to testify in favor of the Charmer. I have never experienced such a situation. Even though I was going to testify in favor of my husband, the thought of being on the witness stand terrified me. When I was called to the witness stand, I performed horribly. I mentally blanked out each time and could not remember anything. I was terrified as if I were on trial and it was me who was going to jail. Dealing with the trial and all the other responsibilities, I was completely stressed out. I did not have the mental capacity to work full-time. I had to take a paid leave of absence from full-time work because I could not handle the emotional stress.

At this phase in my life, my mother was now at a place where she wanted to do the right thing. She had been in rehab and was now in a place where she wanted to overcome her addiction. God knew I needed someone by my side to help support me through this. Since my mom was trying to get her life right, I allowed her to come and live with me. This was the beginning of my mother and I rebuilding our mother-daughter relationship.

I was happy to have my mother by my side for support. However, I was still very depressed and sad. I cried and prayed constantly. I asked God, "Why do I have to continue to experience the pain in these relationships I chose in search of love?" Why do I have to continue to endure things that do not allow me to heal within but continue to add to my layers of feeling broken? Why was I so blind, failing to realize the love I should have been searching for was the love of God?

God's love for me was always present in my life, even though I failed many times at acknowledging it. Even though many of my decisions placed me in these unfortunate relationships, God's love for me was ever-present and a steadfast force in my life. He was always there, providing His love and support through the relationships I had no control over and the bad relationships I chose. Isaiah 54:10 (NIV) states, "though the mountains be shaken, and hills be removed, yet my unfailing love for you will not be shaken nor my covenant of peace be removed, says the Lord, who has compassion from you."

Because the Charmer accepted a plea deal, his trial ended. Unfortunately, he was sent back to prison. The result was unfortunate; however, I was relieved that I no longer had to endure the overwhelming stress this trial had placed on me. However, I was in debt from all my financial obligations. I did have the financial burden of our used car lot business, the rental properties, and my household expenses. The money from the car lot and the rental properties was not enough to survive after expenses were paid. I was at risk of my home foreclosure and my cars being repossessed.

Though I did not know how to maintain it, I was reminded of the word of God. Philippians 4:19 (ESV) declares, "And my God will supply every need of yours according to his riches in glory in Christ Jesus." I went back to work full-time to pay off some of my expenses. As much as I tried to maintain my used car lot business and the rental properties, I had to face the reality that these expenses were too much for me to maintain. I eventually let the car lot and the rental properties go. My credit was ruined after I let go of the car lot and the rental properties. However, the blessing in disguise was that I could prevent my home from going into foreclosure and my cars from being repossessed. God provided for me in ways that allowed me to keep what I needed and let go of the things that were a hindrance. He also made it possible for me to get out of debt. There was no way I would have accomplished getting out of debt in my strength, "For nothing would be impossible for God" (Luke 1:37, ESV).

Even though things had improved financially, I was still emotionally broken. At this point, I was very angry that I had endured 11 years of the Charmer's infidelity and then had to deal with the consequences of his illegal activity. Additionally, I was angry that I could have been indicted for what he was doing and was not involved in it. If I had been indicted, I would have lost my nursing license and would not have been able to work. The worst consequence is that I could have lost my children if I had been charged with this crime. I became so angry with myself, knowing I allowed all of this to happen because of my strong desire to be in a loving relationship.

The trial ends and forgiveness begins

As I continued to pray to God, He placed it in my spirit to not be angry and forgive Him. Romans 12:17–21 says, "Repay no one evil for evil but give thought to do what is honorable in the sight of all. If possible, so far as it depends on you, live peaceably with all. Beloved, never avenge yourselves, but leave it to the wrath of God, for it is written, 'Vengeance is mine, I will repay, says the Lord.' To the contrary, "if your enemy is hungry, feed him; if he is thirsty, give him something to drink; for by so doing you will heap burning coals on his head. Do not be overcome by evil, but overcome evil with good." As I continued to pray, God led me to a few more scriptures on forgiveness. Matthew 6:14–16 states, "for if you forgive other people when they sin against you, your heavenly Father will also forgive you. But if you do not forgive others their sins, your Father will not forgive you of your sins." Ephesians 4:31–32 (NIV) states, "get rid of all bitterness, rage, and anger, brawling and slander, along with every form of malice. Be kind and compassionate to one another, forgiving each other, just as in Christ God forgave you."

God is a loving and forgiving Father. If I wanted to heal from my brokenness, I had to know God's love and love as He loves. My healing from brokenness began by praying and meditating on God's word. Through that process, I learned how to forgive myself for my mistakes and others. I forgave the Charmer for all that he put me through. After I forgave him, the Lord placed it on my heart that it was time to let go. Eight months after the Charmer was sentenced, I filed for divorce. He did not agree with getting divorced, but he did not want to put me through anything further and peacefully granted me the divorce.

When I look back at this situation, I recognize that I would have avoided all these things I endured if I had trusted my spirit when it told me that I was moving too fast. I would have learned a lot about the Charmer early in the relationship. Unfortunately, there was no way I could have known I would be in a situation with severe consequences. My advice to anyone is that if you sense that someone is involved in illegal activity, I strongly suggest you look at how this could negatively impact your life. If I did not have God's love and protection covering me, I would have been searching for love inside a jail cell.

CHAPTER 10

BACK ON THE WRONG PATHWAY

Being divorced for the third time made me feel even worse about myself. For years, I had experienced one bad relationship after another. I did not have any friends, and I was still dealing off and on with the issues I had experienced with my parents when I was younger. Instead of pursuing love and being hit with another disappointment, I began to work more. By working more, it helped me decide to pursue graduate school.

Working a lot and going back to school for my master's degree in nursing and business administration occupied my time for three and a half years. I did not think about dating or want to date after all I had been through. Also, I stayed in my prayer closet, on my knees, praying to God during this time. I did not want to do anything without His presence in my life. "And we know that for those who love God, all things work together for good, for those who are called according to his purpose" (Romans 8:28, ESV).

During my three-and-a-half years in my hiatus from relationships, I was building my relationship with the Lord. I would constantly be in my prayer closet, praying and meditating. Unfortunately, as much as I prayed, I did not pray the right prayers. I did not pray for God to show me His vision for my life. My prayers did not include requests for complete healing and restoration from all factors that contributed to my feelings of brokenness.

In *Happy, Healthy, and Whole* Paula White Cain shares, "until we become healthy, whole, and healed, we will not be happy and cannot give or receive true love from someone." This statement has proven true in my life because I did not apply the principles of God's love in my life and because I did not pray for healing, I could not receive the love I desired, nor could I give the love that others desired from me in my relationships. Since I had not completely healed, I again found myself in another bad relationship.

After dealing with all that I experienced with my third husband, I began to pray to God to send me a man who was only interested in me and made everything about me. Looking back, I should have been praying to God for a man who was made in His image and who loved as God loves. We are reminded, "Beloved, let us love one another, for love is from God, and whoever loves has been born of God and knows God" (1 John 4:7, ESV). Though I got the man I was asking for, I knew he was not sent by God.

Meeting for the first time

One day, after a busy day at work, my coworker and I decided to go out to eat and have a drink. The wait time to be seated at a table was over 30 minutes, so my coworker and I decided to sit at the bar. There were no two empty bar stools side by side. However, a young man was sitting nearby and offered his bar stool so my friend and I could sit together.

The young man eventually found another bar stool and sat next to my co-worker and me. He began initiating conversation, but I was not interested at first. My co-worker, who sat between us, was trying to engage us in conversation. My co-worker felt that after three and a half years of not dating, it was time for me to start dating again. To allow the young man and I time to talk, she excused herself from the bar so that we could talk.

He gave me his life story in such a short time. My first thought was that this man was not the one for me. Regardless of my initial thought, we continued to talk, and after dinner, he walked me to my car. We exchanged numbers before leaving, and he called me that night to ensure I made it home safely. However, I did not speak to him until a week later. I decided to call him because my coworker and I were discussing investing, and she thought it would be a good idea to call. My co-worker encouraged me to call him because he was an accountant at a bank. So, I called him, and from this day forward, we developed a friendship that led to a romantic relationship.

Initially, I did not think he was the man for me because he was a tall, young, white man. I have never dated outside my race before, nor have I dated anyone younger than me. Though I felt this way, he was handsome with green eyes. His appearance reminded me of one of my favorite R&B singers, Jon B. First, we just had conversations over the phone, but as we talked more, I became more interested in him. During our phone conversations, he was very nurturing and affectionate, and he always discussed how he would take care of me in a domestic capacity. I will call this young man the Domestic because he always talked about caring for me by cooking for me, having my bath water ready when I got home and being attentive to all my needs.

Even though he talked about how much he would care for me, I believed we connected by discussing all the dysfunction in our lives. He was just as broken as I was; he, too, did not feel he received the love he desired from his parents; he felt unloved and unworthy, and he had two failed marriages. In *Happy, Healthy, and Whole,* Paula White Cain also shares, "You cannot give others wholeness if you are broken. To give something, you must have it to give. To love others, we must first love ourselves. Relationships that function the best start with two people who are healthy, whole, and complete."

Domestic and I spoke on the phone for over a month before we decided to go on our first date. The date was okay; we talked and had dinner. After the second date, I again felt he was not the one for me. He acted like a wimpy little kid, and I decided to break it off with him. When I tried to break up with him, he called and texted my phone non-stop. He made me feel bad for not allowing time to give us a chance. I gave in to him and decided to give him another chance. Unfortunately for me, this was just the beginning of the signs of his neediness and codependency.

The relationship Domestic and I were in a codependent dysfunctional relationship. In *Happy, Healthy, and Whole* Paula White-Cain describes codependency as "repeating sick cycles and patterns that leads to people doing just about anything to feel needed and loved." I still strongly desired to be in a loving relationship, so I settled for him. We both wanted to be in a loving relationship. However, I believe his desires were greater than mine. He wanted more from me than what I had to give. I had not fully accepted and understood God's love for me. Additionally, I was not healed from all the rejection and pain I had experienced over the years that led to my brokenness.

What he wanted and expected from me felt like I was carrying 300 lbs. of extra weight. He began behaving like he needed me and could not function without me. Initially, he did shower me with all the affection he originally spoke of when we first met. However, he wanted us to be around each other all the time. The relationship became very unhealthy early on; he did not give me any space to breathe or do anything without him.

You do not know how to love yourself until you know the love of God. I loved God, but I had not learned how to love myself. I had not grown enough in His word to understand the foundation of true love that would lead me to love myself. Because I did not love myself, I continued to pick the same types of people who just looked different. I did not discover who I was in Christ; therefore, my circumstances or relationships did not change, and I continued to be a part of dysfunctional relationships.

I do or I don't

Domestic and I had many conversations about allowing space and time to grow. We worked through it, and after two years of dating, we decided to get married. I wish I could say that it was true love, but I settled for him and fell in love with the fact that he would do anything to show his love and affection for me, so because of his affection for me, I decided to marry him.

Domestic and I had a beautiful destination wedding. We stayed in a five-star hotel with a private pool on the balcony overlooking the ocean and had our butler that catered to our every need. Our wedding was in a secluded area on the beach. Everything was blissful except for the person I was marrying. Domestic complained and whined about every little thing to the point that we argued the entire time. He turned what was supposed to be the most beautiful and romantic moment into a horrible experience.

Right before we went away to get married, I was offered a job opportunity in another city. This was a great opportunity to advance my career and a great chance for Domestic and I to start over and grow our relationship alone as newlyweds since we were living with my sons and my mother. Domestic was looking to transfer to a bank in the new city or find a job at another bank, but Domestic was unable to transfer or find a new job in the new city. He requested a medical leave of absence from his current job to allow him time to find another job as well as give him time to seek the necessary medical treatment he needed. He injured his back when he was younger. Because he did not receive the needed medical treatment when he first injured his back, his injury led to him developing chronic issues and debilitating conditions over time.

I thought moving to a new city would be a fresh start for us. We had moved to a new city, I had a good-paying job, and Domestic was given time off to seek medical attention. We knew he would eventually find a new job or transfer to another bank in the new city. Unfortunately, this did not turn out how I expected. I became the sole provider. I had the financial responsibilities of my expenses back home in the old city and our expenses in the new city. He gave every excuse one could think of as to why he could not find a job. In reality, he did not want to work anymore. I believe he developed the mindset because I could take care of him and all of our expenses because I had a good-paying job.

Once Domestic's leave from work ended, he had to either return to his old position in the old city, which was only three hours away or quit. He decided to quit his job, and unfortunately, he did not try to find another one. He stated that he couldn't find any job opportunities in the city we were in.

It became difficult to maintain all the financial responsibilities. Back home, my family moved out of my home because the plan was to sell it. Since we had not placed the home on the market to be sold, I still had to pay the mortgage. I had to pay my mortgage back home and my rent, along with all the other expenses in the city we live in.

Before he decided to quit his job and go back home, I suggested that, until he is able to transfer or find another job, he could stay at the house during the week to work and commute to the apartment on weekends. The drive between the cities was only three hours. This may not have been the best solution, but I believe families do what is necessary to maintain until situations improve. However, after saying that, he became very offended and could not understand why I would want him to be away from me. In my mind, couples do whatever is necessary to maintain, which might include working in another city to help provide for the household. Since he did not agree with us being apart, he quit his job.

Since he was not working, I suggested he return home and make minor repairs to the house so we could list it for sale. He thought this was a good idea. He did not mind commuting back and forth to make repairs on a home, but he did not want to commute back and forth to go to work. How backward was this? But I went along with it. I do not know what I was thinking when I suggested he go to the house to make the minor repairs needed. He completely made things worse financially for me. He turned minor repairs into major repairs. To fix what he messed up, it would take professionals to repair my home. I did not have the additional money for these repairs. This was an added burden because I could not put my house on the market for sale, and I had to continue to pay the mortgage.

I was heavily burdened; I could not understand how I had a good job but was constantly broke. To add to my stress and burden, he began to display characteristics of someone addicted to prescription pain medications. When he initially injured his back, he did not receive therapy but was given medications. Over time, he became dependent on those medications for his back injury. I believe his dependency turned into an addiction. Since we were in the new city, he began displaying signs of addiction; from my past, I was very aware of those signs.

Since Domestic did not work, he did not have any money. He would take money out of the bank as soon as my check was deposited and do other things with the money. He had no reason to do this because he was not paying any bills. He would also leave when I got home and stay out all night. He would claim that he would stay at an all-night coffee house to read.

As Domestic's behavior became more and more unstable, I continued to pray and ask God to get me out of this situation. I tried to kick him out of the apartment, but I could not kick Domestic out of the apartment because both of our names were on the lease. I had to endure living with him until the lease was up, which was another six months. I informed him that he needed to develop a plan for his life because I was moving on without him when the lease was up. He did not take me seriously until he realized I was making plans without him. Oh, but God! He continued to provide for me, "and my God will meet all your needs according to the riches of his glory in Christ Jesus" (Philippians 4:19, NIV).

Three months before the lease was up, I received a promotion from my job. With the extra money, I could begin the repairs on my home. The plan was that once the repairs were complete, my family would move back into my home and begin to help pay the mortgage. Until the repairs were complete, I would travel home on the weekends. Domestic finally realized that I was moving on after the lease was up in a few months. At this point, I was still unsure of his plans and how he was going to move forward. And then it happened: one weekend, when I returned home, I came to an empty apartment. Domestic had left and taken everything with him.

Most of the furniture in the apartment was his. I had left all my furniture back at my home. However, he was very petty and took items like dish towels and the paper napkin holder. He even took the $5,000 mattress that I had purchased for his back, which made me furious. I was so upset about how he went about this situation. I called him, but he did not answer, so I was angry. God reminded me that the things he took were material items that could be replaced. He reminded me that I should be thankful that he left in a manner that did not cause any harm to himself or me. I did not hear from Domestic after the day I returned home and found the apartment empty; he fled back to the state where his parents lived.

After everything I had endured with Domestic and my other failed relationships, I was again devastated, disappointed, and heartbroken. How could I have allowed myself to enter another bad relationship? I continued to pray to God, asking Him to speak to me and tell me why I kept making the same bad choices. I prayed and asked God to heal me from all the rejection and heartaches I have experienced over the years that have led to my brokenness.

Through it all, God continued to show His love to me. What was meant to be evil turned out to be beneficial to me. I was encouraged by the book of Romans, which says, "And we know that for those who love God all things work together for good" (Romans 8:28, ESV). As I continued to pray and work through my healing process, God allowed things to work in my favor financially once again. Through His provision, the repairs on my home were complete, and my family was able to move back into my home and assist in paying the mortgage. My family's ability to assist with my mortgage was a great relief for me financially, and God continued to bless me financially. Several months after my family moved back into my home, I was blessed with a job opportunity that would allow me to move back home with my family. God is good all the time.

I was happy to be back home. My family and I were in a good place. My mother had been sober for nine years at the time. We all lived in my home, supporting and loving each other as a family. Also, I was financially better; my finances improved, considering I did not have expenses in two different cities. Even though I was in a good place with my finances and family, I was still emotionally broken. I was still very broken from all the layers of abandonment, rejection, and love loss I had experienced over the years.

To add to this, I was still furious about the situation with the Domestic. I filed for divorce; however, divorcing him was difficult. He was in another state, so attempting to serve him divorce papers was complicated. His parents always covered for him and said he was not there. The attorney and I tried to contact him but were unsuccessful. I had not spoken to him since he disappeared from the apartment. After several failed attempts to locate Domestic, my attorney was finally able to proceed with the divorce proceedings. It took over nine months for the divorce to be finalized after I initially filed for the divorce.

I was furious that I married Domestic and had to put up with everything he put me through, as well as the length of time it took for me to divorce him. As I continued to pray, the Lord led me to the following scripture to release me from my angriness: "Let no corrupting talk come out of your mouths, but only such as is good for building up, as fits the occasion, that it may give grace to those who hear. And do not grieve the Holy Spirit of God, by whom you were sealed for the day of redemption. Let all bitterness and wrath and anger and clamor and slander be put away from you, along with all malice. Be kind to one another, tenderhearted, forgiving one another, as God in Christ forgave you" (Ephesians 4:29–32, ESV).

Forgiving and letting go were not easy, but reading and meditating on God's word helped me get to a place where I could truly begin to heal from being broken. During my healing process, I was able to forgive Domestic. I began to understand he was just as broken as I was from all of his past heartaches from being in bad relationships and feeling unloved by his parents. During my healing process, my divorce was finalized. I was happy to be divorced but depressed from having been in another failed marriage.

CHAPTER 11

THE PATHWAY TO GOD'S LOVE

Experiencing one bad relationship after another can leave anyone feeling broken and unloved. That is just where my experiences led me. I have just experienced my fourth failed marriage. I'd had enough of going down the wrong path in search of true love. I decided to get on the path of learning God's love and how to love myself. "But when the goodness and loving kindness of God our Savior appeared, he saved us, not because of works done by us in righteousness, but according to his own mercy, by the washing of regeneration and renewal of the Holy Spirit" (Titus 3:4-5, NIV).

I could not figure out how I kept getting into the same situations with different people. I was praying to God and talking to Him regularly, but I could not understand how I kept becoming involved in these unhealthy relationships. Was God not listening to me when I prayed to Him or was I not listening to God when he spoke to me? It is obvious that I was not listening to God. Time after time God revealed to me how much He loved me, and He was by my side through everything. However, I did not acknowledge His love for me, nor did I prioritize God like the scripture stated. "But seek first the kingdom of God and his righteousness, and all these things will be added to you" (Matthew 6:33, ESV).

Why did it take me so long down the wrong pathway before acknowledging and discovering God's love for me? Why did it take me so long to love and trust God enough to guide me in overcoming past rejection, abandonment, and heartaches? I needed to learn to trust in God as Proverbs says: "Trust in the Lord with all your heart and do not lean on your own understanding. In all your ways acknowledge him and he will make straight your path" (Proverbs 3:5–6, ESV).

As I pondered the previous questions, I realized several things. First, in the beginning, I did not truly allow God into my heart, nor did I ask Him to show me what true love was. When I used to pray to God, I would pray for someone to love me the way I thought true love was in the beginning. I did not pray, asking God to show me His definition of true love. I did not acknowledge God's love or how much He truly loved me. I never prayed to God for healing and restoration from the pain and rejection after each failed relationship or the abandonment I felt from my parents. I did not pray to God, asking for guidance in loving thy self or knowing thy self-worth. Because I did not seek God first and pray for the right things, there is no wonder why I continued to go down the wrong path in searching for true love.

According to Psalm 32:8 (NIV), acknowledging God first "will instruct you and teach you in the way you should go; I will counsel you with my eye upon you."

After my fourth marriage, I really took time to know God by meditating on His word constantly. God loved me, and He continued to reference His love for me throughout the Bible. In Romans, the scripture says, "No, in all these things we are more than conquerors through him who loved us. For I am convinced that neither death nor life, neither angels nor demons, neither the present nor the future, nor any powers, neither height nor depth, nor anything else in all creation, will be able to separate us from the love of God that is in Christ Jesus or Lord" (Roman 8:37–39, NIV). God demonstrated His love for me in every circumstance of my life.

Through His words, I began to recognize how much He loved me, and I began to love Him unconditionally. The love I have been searching for all these years has been with me all my life. As I began to acknowledge and receive God's love through His word, he showed me how to love and value myself. Meditating on God's word gave me the confidence to know that I am fearfully and wonderfully made and that I am not what the world tried to convince me to believe about myself. I began to love myself and respect myself enough not to continue to involve myself in relationships that were not worthy of me.

God continued to demonstrate His love for me by restoring my family relationships. My mother and my father have both been sober for over fifteen years. The bond between my mother, father, and I is closer than ever. My mother and father are divorced, but they are best friends. My oldest son and I are closer than ever. We respect, love, and understand each other. I am also very proud of the man he has become and the loving father he is to his children. My youngest son also continues to grow into the man God is calling him to be. Though my pathway was long, I finally have discovered a love like no other, which is God's love!

A Love Like No Other

In summary, I have encountered many experiences while trying to find true love and happiness. Over the years, I experienced neglect, abandonment from my parents, rejection from my friends, and heartaches and disappointment in my romantic relationships. All these experiences have led me to feel unloved and broken. The blessing in all my unfortunate experiences is that I discovered the true love of God. God's love for me healed me from my brokenness, and I became whole. His love is like no other love I have experienced. Because of his love for me, I can love myself and others. His love for me has given me the ability to desire a love that represents his kind of love.

I feel loved; I am full of love, and I am at peace. I am happy, complete and whole. However, I am still open to finding a loving relationship that is centered around the love of God. If I do not find that loving relationship that is centered around the love of God, I will be okay. I have discovered God's love, which is a love like no other. Now, I will not settle for anything less.

THE AUTHOR

Lakisha Young was born in Houston, Texas. She is the only child and is the mother of two sons and has six grandchildren. Lakisha has a Master in Science of Nursing and a Master in Business Administration. Lakisha has been a registered nurse for 23 years. Lakisha is also a certified life coach, a new author and a business owner.

Lakisha has a heart after God. She is most passionate about discipleship and ministering and mentoring young adults. Lakisha's mission is to empower a generation and teach about the love of God. Lakisha has endured and overcame many obstacles in life. She overcame the many obstacles she endured by her faith, trust and her love for Christ Jesus. After true healing, God blessed her with a fulfilling and loving relationship with a Godly man. Lakisha is happily married to Pastor Ramon Jones.

A Love Like No Other

A Love Like No Other

A Love Like No Other

www.ingramcontent.com/pod-product-compliance
Lightning Source LLC
LaVergne TN
LVHW051847080426
835512LV00018B/3122